The Li

DALI

Catherine de Duve

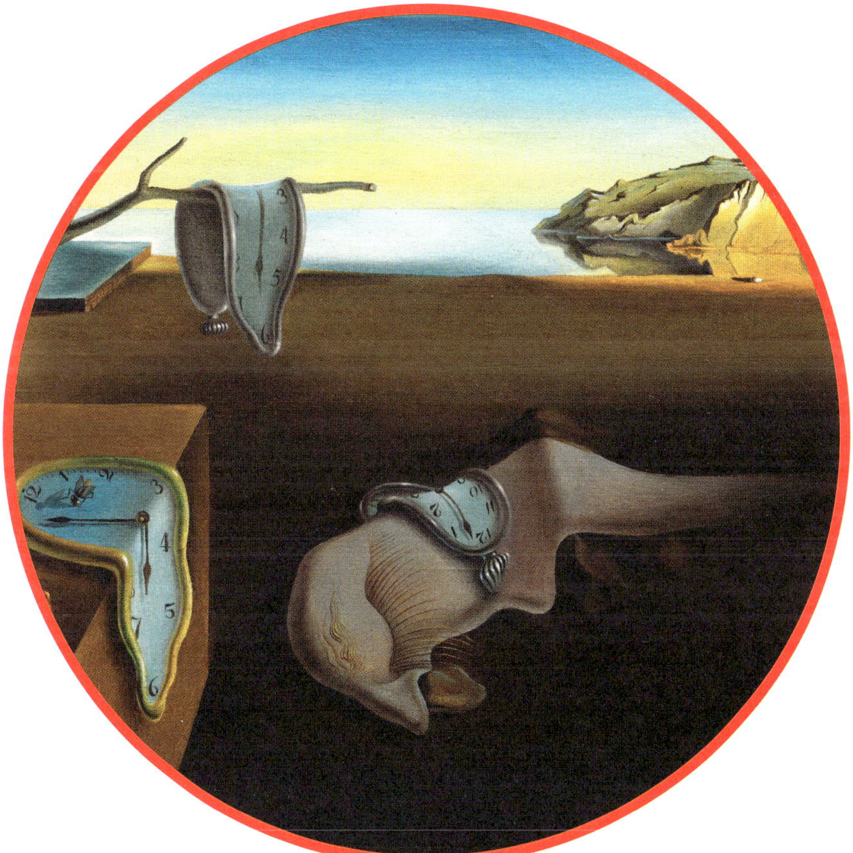

Discover the life and masterpieces
of the famous Surrealist painter

KATE'ART
EDITIONS

The world of

Salvador Dalí loved the area where he grew up: Figueres, Cadaqués and Portlligat, in Catalonia, Spain. Everything here inspired him! The sea and the large, animal-shaped rocks... He opened up the drawers of his mind, where all his memories were stored, and painted these memories throughout his lifetime.

Portlligat

Cadaqués

Figueres

Castle of Púbol

Salvador Dalí

Dalí

Family

Salvador Dalí was born on May 11th 1904 in Figueres, a small town near Barcelona in the province of Girona, Spain.

His father, Salvador Dalí Cusí, was a notary, and his mother, Felipa Domènech Ferrés, spoiled him. As a child, he could do everything he wanted: he could draw, dress up – as a king with his gold crown and cape – even show off… but he wasn't allowed into the kitchen. Was this why, aged six, he wanted to be a cook?

First name

His parents gave him the same first name as his big brother Salvador (1901-1903), who had died a few months before Dalí was born. They overprotected him and saw him as the reincarnation of their older son. Salvador had a little sister, Anna Maria, four years younger than him. But he was king of the house!

Meet Salvador Dalí's family

His father, Salvador

His mother, Felipa

Salvador

His sister, Anna Maria

Cadaqués

The Dalí family spent their holidays
in their house on Llanera beach, at Cadaqués.

Look at the little port of Cadaqués.
Find the church, the arches and the boats.
What are the women carrying?

Budding genius

Childhood

Aged four, Salvador started primary school. He was shy and rebellious, didn't work well and changed school. He learnt French and took private drawing lessons. He was very gifted. At a family friends' house, Salvador discovered art. He admired Impressionist paintings and began to paint. At home, he set up a small studio in the attic.

1918

First exhibition

Aged 14, Dalí took part in a collective exhibition at the Figueres municipal theatre (the future Dalí Theatre-Museum). The public admired his precocious talent.

At the age of eight, he copied the *Venus de Milo* – there was a picture of the sculpture on his pencil case.

Later, Dalí copied the antique sculpture again, and added a set of drawers to her body.

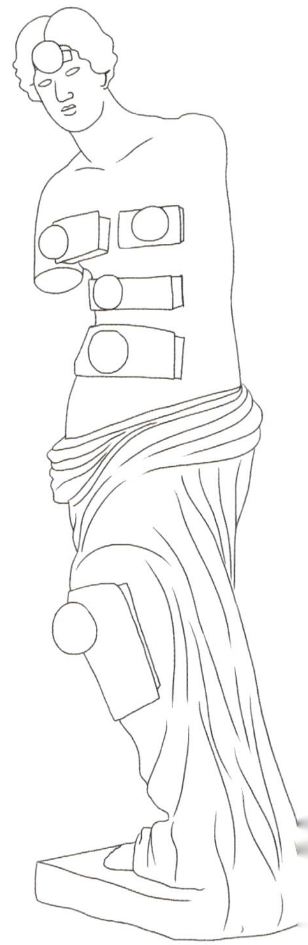

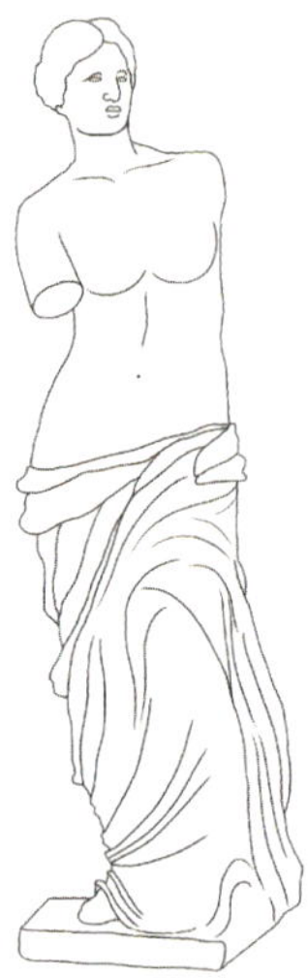

Colour in the two Venuses. Dalí's Venus has drawers with pompom handles, to store his childhood memories in.

Moustache

Academy

Dalí wanted to be a painter. In 1922, he entered the San Fernando Royal Academy of Fine Arts, in Madrid. His father wanted him to be a teacher. Dalí visited the Prado museum, where he admired the paintings by Velázquez*.

At the student centre he met **Luis Buñuel** and **Federico García Lorca**, who became his friends. Dalí wrote poems and texts about art. He convinced himself that he was a genius. As he didn't hesitate to criticise his teachers, the young artist was asked to leave.

Dali the dandy

Dalí liked to be elegant and to dress up.
At the academy, he wore a black velvet suit, kept his hair long and used makeup (he whitened his skin and outlined his eyes in black).

He had a moustache.
His moustache acted as an 'aerial', a radar which captured his ideas as they floated through the air.

Colour in Dali's suit and moustache.

* To find out more, take a look at *The Little Velázquez*, by the same publisher

Summer holidays

Studio with sea view

Dalí set up a studio in a first-floor room of the family holiday home. What did he paint? He painted the sea, the horizon, the rocks, the light, the boats... and also self-portraits and pictures of his sister Anna Maria, who acted as his model. Dalí was trying to find a style of his own.

In this picture he paints in the style of the Impressionists*, with small brushstrokes and thick paint which catches the light. What a vibrant effect!

Canvas on the easel

Palette of paints

What time is it in the studio? Where's the sun? What can we see through the window?

Canvasses drying on the wall

Light flooding into the room

 * To find out more, take a look at *Long Live Impressionism and Pointillism!*, in the same collection

Paris

First visit to Paris

In April 1926, Dalí visited Paris for the first time. He met the painter **Pablo Picasso*** and went to the Louvre Museum, where he discovered the works of the old masters, such as Vermeer's* *The Lacemaker*. He later (in 1955) copied this painting, 'but better', as he then declared.

Dalí's favourite painting: *The Lacemaker*, 1669, by Vermeer

Films

Dalí returned to Paris in 1929 to make his first short film. The Spanish painter **Joan Miró*** introduced him to the Surrealists, a group of artists led by **André Breton**.

1929

AN ANDALUSIAN DOG

In 1929, Dalí and his friend **Buñuel** produced their first film (16 minutes long): *An Andalusian Dog*. It was inspired by one of Buñuel's dreams.

What surprising images! An eyeball is cut with a razor, ants crawl out of the palm of a hand, which then becomes an armpit, then a sea urchin, etc.

1930

The Golden Age

The second film he made with Buñuel, *The Golden Age*, was banned by the censors until 1981.

*To find out more, take a look at *The Little Picasso*, *The Little Miró* and *The Little Vermeer* in the same collec

Gala

A Surrealist summer in Cadaqués

In the summer of 1929, Dalí was visited by the gallerist Camille Goemans, by Luis Buñuel accompanied by **René and Georgette Magritte***, and by the poet **Paul Éluard** and his wife Gala. The small group of Surrealists spent their holidays in Cadaqués. Dalí fell madly in love with Gala, whose real name was **Elena Ivanovna Diakonova** (1894-1982).

Gala was Russian, beautiful and ten years older than him. She became his muse, who inspired him. From then on, they were inseparable. Dalí's father did not accept his provocative art, nor his relationship with a married woman. Salvador was no longer welcome at Cadaqués.

Piece Gala's fragmented face back together.

Dalí became interested in the sciences, more specifically in atomic physics. In 1952, he painted *Galatea of the Spheres.* In this portrait, the artist seems to be trying to show the disintegration of atoms.

*To find out more, take a look at *The Little Magritte*, in the same collection

Surrealist

Dalí painted this Surrealist picture, which he showed at his first individual exhibition, at the Goemans Gallery in Paris.

What is Surrealism?

Surrealism is based on the world of dreams and of the unconscious (Freud). The Surrealists practised 'pure psychic automatism' (Breton). What does that mean? They tried to free their thoughts from the control exercised by reason, with no regard for aesthetic or moral concerns.

My mystical paradise

This face in profile was inspired by the shape of one of the rocks at Cap de Creus near Cadaqués.

'This landscape is a permanent source of inspiration for me'

Over to you! Write down, without thinking, the thoughts in your head.

Avida Dollars

The first few creative years were very difficult.
The Dalís had to find patrons to help them financially.

Years later (in 1940), **André Breton**, the leader of the Surrealists, thought that Dalí was too fond of money. He gave him a nickname: **Avida Dollars**. It was an anagram of his name (the letters of his name mixed up!). Dalí's reaction was surprising. He happily declared:

'I am the richest painter in the world!'

How does this picture make you feel?
Find these shapes used by Dalí:

Lion

Pebbles, grass or multicoloured eyelashes, hook

Giant cricket and ants

A rock at Cap de Creus

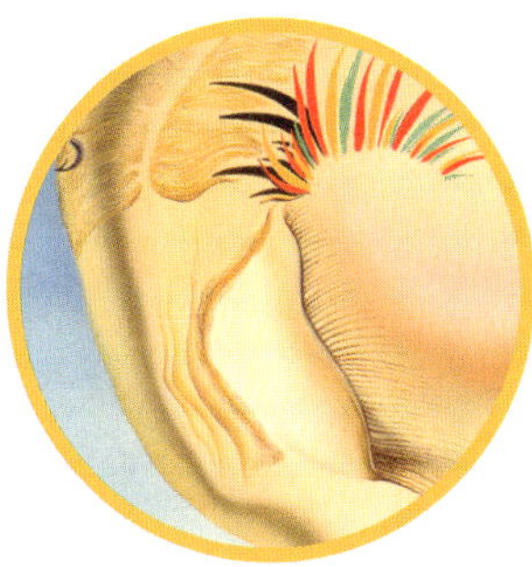

Frown, closed eye and long eyelashes

Stylised architecture and holes

Paranoiac critical

In 1930, Dalí invented a creative process, the **paranoiac critical method**. In this method, the creator moves on spontaneously from one thing to a series of images, generated by 'delirious associations and interpretations'. By means of these 'delirious' associations, a horse becomes a woman, then a lion, etc. These are double or triple images.

Can you see a double image in the shape of this rock at Cap de Creus?

Haunting images

His childhood memories resurfaced in his consciousness: a whole new storehouse of images to fill his strange compositions.

Crutches

Ants

Discover the images which obsessed Dalí.

Egg

Elephants with insects'legs

Hallucination

In 1931, Dalí painted *Hallucination: six images of Lenin on a grand piano*. In a dark room, a piano keyboard is lit up by six small heads. They are heads of the Russian Soviet leader, **Lenin** (1870-1924), who came to power in Russia in 1917.

The leader of the Surrealists was not happy with this picture. The eccentric Dalí was asked to come and explain himself, but instead, he just acted as a clown. He was excluded from the Surrealist group in 1939.

'The difference between the Surrealists and me is that I'm a Surrealist'

What's Surrealist about this picture?
Find the ants, the cherries and the safety pins.

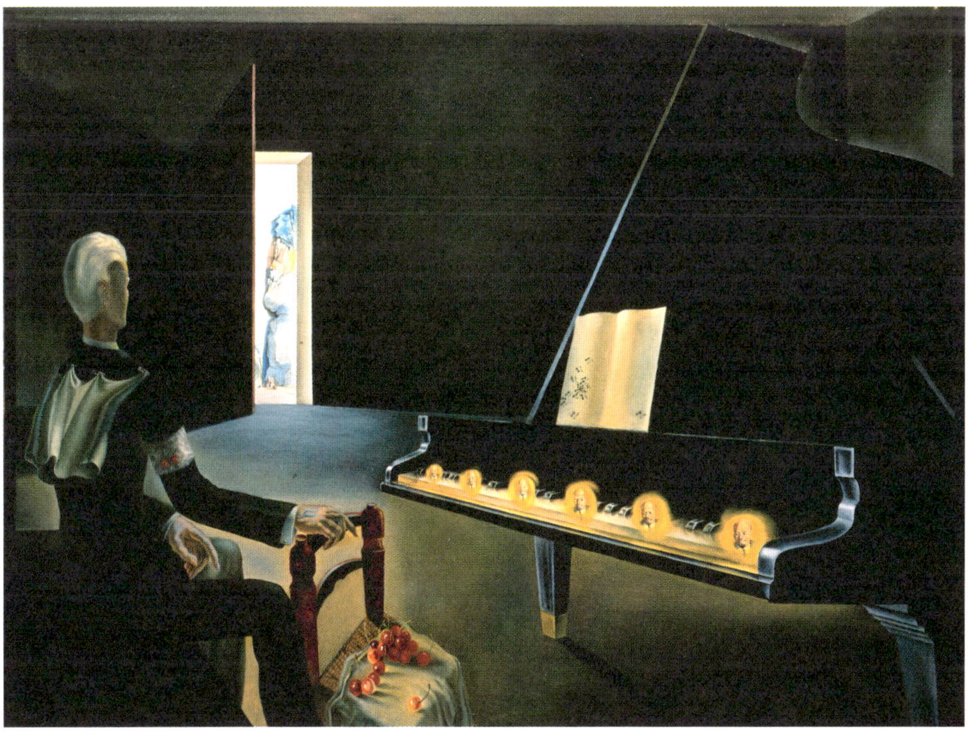

Soft clocks

Camembert

At the age of 27, Dalí found his own style. He produced polished, complex compositions inspired by his dreams and fantasies.

One day, after tasting a runny camembert, he had the idea of painting soft clocks, melting like cheese. Using a magnifying glass, he painted a mysterious landscape, *The Persistence of Memory*. This picture was bought by an American gallerist.

Where are we? What time is it?
How many clocks can you count?

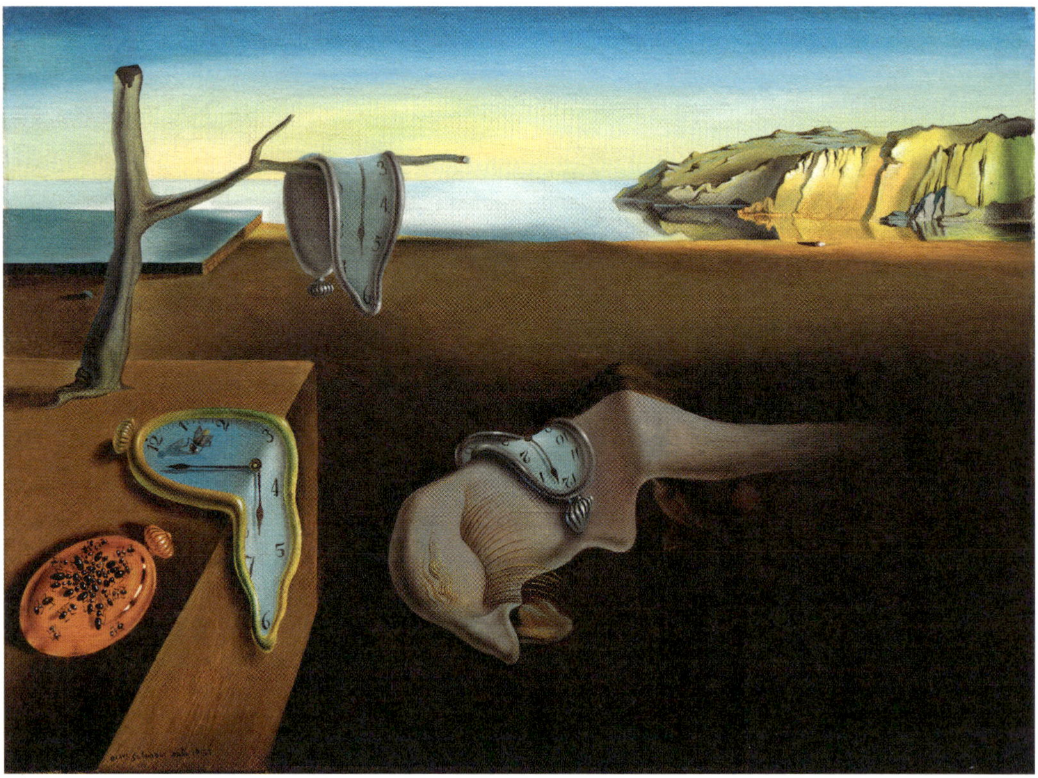

Ants

One day, Dalí found a wounded bat covered in 'frenetic ants'.
In his art, ants would represent the terror of death (putrefaction) which he felt from that time onwards.

Look closely at the *Persistence of Memory*. Find these details in the painting. What do they mean?

Hard and soft

The clock (hard) has melted (soft). It's hanging softly from a branch.

Time

Ants are swarming over the clock. They symbolise death (decomposition). The fly, however, symbolises life.

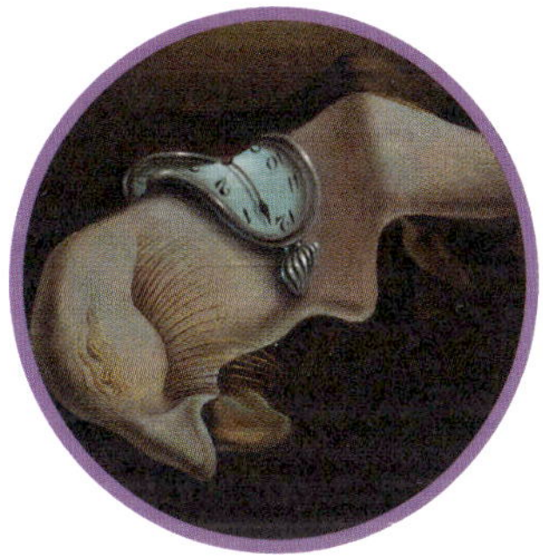

Dalí's face

In profile: is he dreaming, or changing into an insect?

Steep cliffs

Cap de Creus, Costa Brava, in Catalonia.

Sea and sky

The blue sea (a cold colour), the dark beach and the horizon with its golden sky (warm colours).

Desert landscape

A dead tree, a wide plank, a pebble, the distant horizon.

Narcissus

Who's in love with Narcissus?

In *Metamorphoses*, the Greek poet Ovid tells the myth of Narcissus. Narcissus was a proud, very handsome young man and a heart-breaker. While he was drinking from a spring, he caught sight of his reflection in the water and fell in love with his own image. 'Alas!', he lamented, as he spent day after day gazing at his reflection. In despair, he weakened and died. White flowers grew there, with yellow hearts. They now bear his name: narcissi.

Find the myth of Narcissus in *Metamorphosis of Narcissus*, painted in 1937.

Double images

Narcissus is kneeling in the water. In despair, his head on his knee, he seems to disappear.

On his right, a blue hand, which has turned to stone, emerges from the ground. It's holding an egg, from which a white flower is growing. Isn't this Narcissus, turning into a flower?

Meeting with Freud

On July 19th 1938, in London, Dalí met **Sigmund Freud** (1856-1939), the founder of psychoanalysis. Dalí drew two small sketches of him, as he explained his theories on paranoia – while Freud looked at the picture without reacting. Freud then declared 'I have never seen a more complete example of a Spaniard. What a fanatic!' Dalí was delighted.

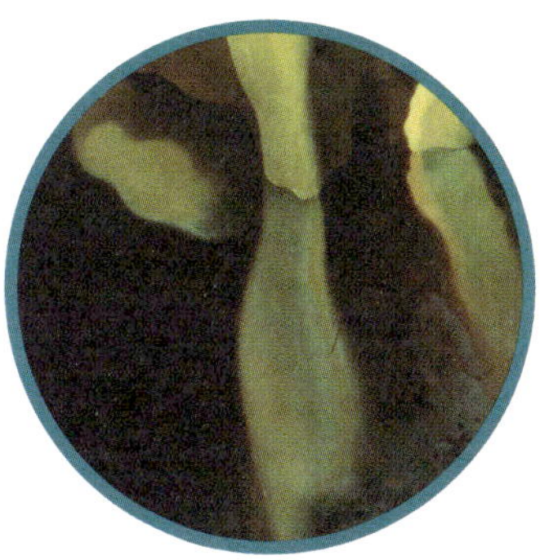

In this picture, find the identical shapes or double images.

New York

America!

In 1936, the Civil War broke out in Spain; this was followed by the Second World War (1939-1945). Salvador and Gala moved to New York. There Dalí took on new projects: advertisements, hats - with the stylist **Elsa Schiaparelli**, department store windows, scenery for ballets, a film set for **Hitchcock**, and even a plan to produce an animated film with **Walt Disney**.

First retrospective

In 1941, Dalí had his first retrospective exhibition at New York's Museum of Modern Art (MoMA), at the same time as **Miró***.

Melted self-portrait

On the pedestal of the melted mask, you can read 'Soft self portrait'. Dalí called it a 'glove' of himself.

Dali

Compare Dali's self-portrait with the self-portrait by Michelangelo. Can you see any similarities?

Dalí was inspired by a detail from the fresco painted by **Michelangelo*** (1475-1564) in the Vatican's Sistine Chapel, in Rome. A strange self-portrait…

Michelangelo

*To find out more, take a look at *The Little Michelangelo* and *The Little Miró* in the same collection

Find the pedestal, the grilled bacon and Dalí's moustache. How many crutches can you count? What are the ants doing?

Crutch

One day, when he was nine years old, Dalí found a crutch in an attic. It was much better than his royal sceptre! The crutch became his all-purpose magic wand – for repelling, caressing, supporting…

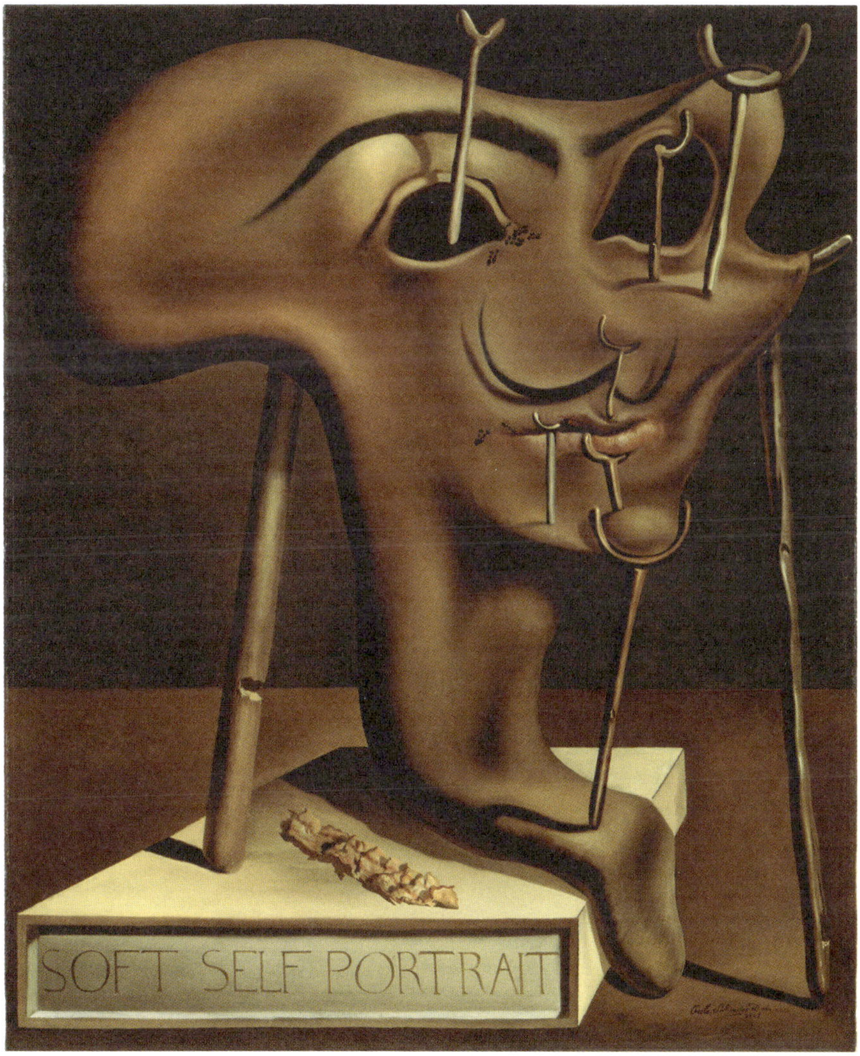

Hello?

Telephone or lobster?

How very surprising! Dalí, who didn't like picking up the phone – he saw it as a threatening object which surprises you by ringing without warning – began to include telephones in his work. Here, the artist combines a telephone with a lobster. This sculpture was shown at the 1938 International Surrealist Exhibition in Paris. He made several versions of this sculpture.

'I don't understand why, in a restaurant, when I order grilled lobster, they never bring me a telephone!'

Over to you!
Design your own Surrealist telephone!

Did you know?

Dalí's favourite dish was lobster with chocolate sauce!

Portlligat

Back from the United States, Gala and Salvador settled in Portlligat, away from Cadaqués. This was where his father was born, and where, as a child, he used to come and play. They extended and decorated their little house. Nearby, the Cap de Creus coast formed a fantasy landscape.

'You can't understand my painting if you don't know Portlligat.'

Cap de Creus

The unusual geology of the area was a constant source of inspiration.
Dalí had visions.
In the rocks he saw profiles and animals: a lion, eagle, camel…

What about you? What can you see in this landscape and in the shapes of the rocks? Compare the photos of Cap de Creus with Dalí's pictures. Can you see any similarities?

Tigers

Dalí was very interested in dreams,
as dreams freely express our unconscious mind.

Interpreting Gala's dream

Gala, like a sleeping Venus, levitates in the air above a flat rocky promontory. The buzzing of a bee, attracted by a floating piece of fruit (a pomegranate), sparks a strange dream…
All around her, the sea is shining like a mirror. The sky is radiant.
The picture is painted in delicate shades of gold and pearly blue.

What is Gala dreaming about?

Find the following items:
Two drops of water
Two pomegranates
A rifle with a bayonet
The rock opposite
Portlligat
The moon
The horizon

How many animals
are there?

Who's eating who?
Find them:
A giant redfish
Two tigers
An elephant
A bee

Elephants

In 1946, Dalí painted *The Temptation of Saint Anthony*.
He entered this painting in a contest organised by a film production company, but the prize was won by the Surrealist artist **Max Ernst**.

How many elephants can you count in this Surrealist picture?

What story is told in this picture?

Saint Anthony, a hermit living in the desert, is hallucinating. He brandishes a cross to fend off his own temptations.
How are these shown?
Strength: a rearing horse.
Lust: an elephant carrying a golden cup, with a naked woman standing on it.

Find the temptations of Saint Anthony.

Procession of elephants
with insects' legs

Obelisk

Woman

Trumpet of fame
named after a Greek goddess

El Escorial
the King of Spain's palace near Madrid

Saint Anthony

Angel

Desert

Rock

Skull
A symbol of death and of redemption from sin

The horse
Strength is represented by a white horse rearing up. The horseshoes are nailed back-to-front onto wooden planks dripping green moss. The horse is baring its teeth in a threatening way.

Pebbles

Mouth

Anthropomorphical jewel

In 1949, Dalí created a brooch in the shape of a plump mouth, *Ruby lips*. The shape of the lips and their red colour reminded him of the pomegranate seeds from his home region.

How many pearl-teeth are there?

Design

Dalí designed this pink sofa to look like the lips of **Mae West**, an American actress of the 1930s. He was fascinated by them.

On a magazine page, using gouache, Dalí painted *Mae West's face which may be used as a Surrealist Apartment.*

Over to you! Imagine a living room with a mouth-sofa, hair-curtains and a nose-fireplace! There it is – your Surrealist apartment.

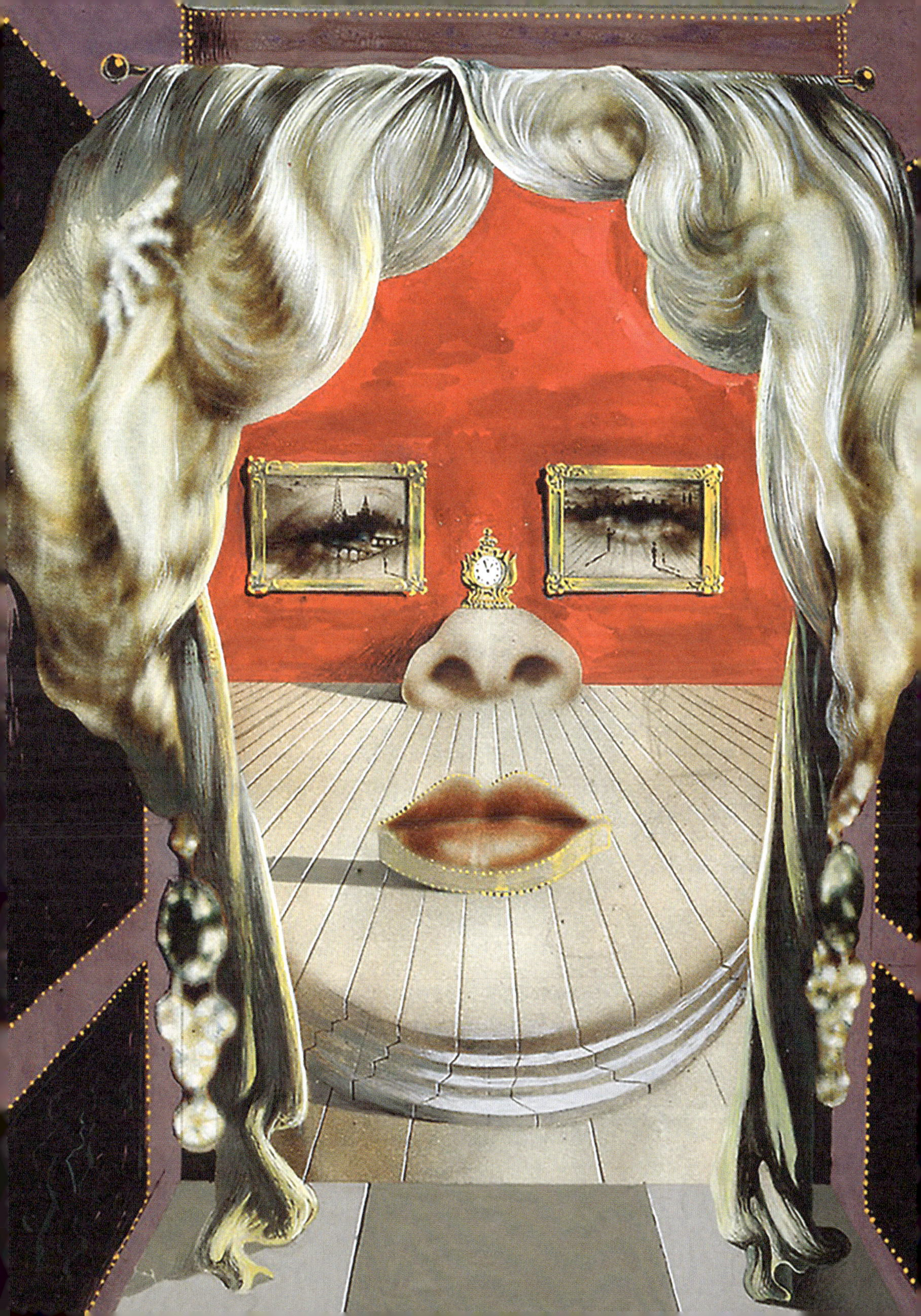

Marquis of Púbol

In the 1930s, Dalí had promised his wife to give her a castle. Forty years later, Gala became the owner of the **Castle of Púbol**. Dalí was allowed to visit, but only with a written invitation from her.

When Gala died in 1982, aged 88, she was buried in the castle crypt. Dalí furnished the throne room. He lived in the castle until the day, in 1984, when fire swept through his bedroom. Badly burnt, he was taken to the hospital and never came back to live in the castle.

Visit Gala's castle and gardens, decorated by Salvador Dalí.

1982

Honorary title

Dalí was given a title by the King of Spain and became a marquis.

On January 23rd 1989, Salvador Dalí died of heart failure in Figueres hospital, aged 84. He was buried in the crypt which he had built for himself under the dome of the Figueres Theatre-Museum.

This museum, the **Dalí Theatre-Museum**, was designed by the artist himself.

'With Picasso, I am the greatest painter of the century'

Salvador Dalí Museum

There is a Salvador Dalí museum in St Petersburg, Florida, USA. It houses the largest Dalí collection: more than 2,100 pieces of art.

Text: Catherine de Duve
Concept and editorial coordination: Kate'Art Editions
Proofreading: Julie Stouffs and Claire Oberst
Translated by: Rachel Cowler

PHOTOGRAPHIC CREDITS:
Brussels: Royal Museums of Fine Arts of Belgium: *The Temptation of Saint Anthony*, 1946: cover, pp. 26-27 | **Canberra: National Gallery of Australia:** *Lobster-Telephone*, 1936: p. 22 © Ian Dagnall Computing / Alamy Banque D'Images | **Chicago: Art Institute of Chicago:** *Venus de Milo with drawers, 1936*: p.6 – *Mae West's face which may be used as a Surrealist apartment,* 1934-35: p.29 | **Figueres: Gala-Salvador Dalí Foundation:** *Gala Placidia (Galatea of the spheres),* 1952: p.11 – *Soft self-portrait with grilled bacon,* 1941: pp.20-21 – *Ruby lips,* 1949: p.28 | **Dalí Theatre-Museum:** *Port Alguer*, c.1923: p.5 | **London: Tate Modern:** *Metamorphosis of Narcissus,* 1937: pp.18-19 | **Madrid: Thyssen-Bornemisza National Museum:** *Face of the Great Masturbator,* 1929*:* pp.12- 13 – *Dream caused by the flight of a bee around a pomegranate a second before waking,* c.1944: pp.24-25 | **New York : Museum of Modern Art:** *The persistence of memory*, 1931: cover, pp.16-17 | **Paris : Musée National d'Art Moderne, Centre Pompidou:** *Hallucination : Six images of Lenin on a grand piano,* 1931: p.15 | **St. Petersburg, Florida: Salvador Dalí Museum:** *Selfportrait in a studio,* c.1919: pp. 8-9

Citations: S. Dalí, Posicío moral del surrealismo, in Hèlix, mars 1930 cité in Dalí : Retrospective 1920-1980, p. 276, CNAC Georges-Pompidou, Paris, 1979: p.7 - Freud: S. Zweig, Correspondance, Paris, Bibliothèque Rivage, 1991, p.24: p.19

With thanks to Mercedes Aznar, Fundació Gala-Salvador Dalí, Philippe Halsman Archive, Géraldine Barbery, Gregory Deswarte, Valerio Fravallo, Olivier de Lathuy and all those involved in the production of this book